AF577039

Sarah's Dream Dress is inspired by the powerful Biblical story of Sarah, which reveals the godly character a girl needs to develop as she shines for Jesus in this world. In a world of instant gratification, we know Sarah's story will teach patience to young ladies.

Read more about Sarah: Genesis 18:1-15; 21:1-7

Sarah's Dream Dress

Written & Compiled
by Bianca Serfontein & Nicola Meyer
Illustrated
by Frances Tomaselli

The Kristen Collection © 2019
Written & Compiled by Bianca Serfontein & Nicola Meyer
Illustrations by Frances Tomaselli
Check Your Heart by Danél van Lill
Bible verses from the New International Version.
Printed in China
All rights reserved
Distributed by iDisciple under license from
The Kristen Collection

ISBN - 9780999281321

www.thekristencollection.com

To:
From:

Sarah rubbed her eyes. She was sure she was dreaming, because she was standing in front of Phia's Boutique. The window display was so beautiful that she stood absolutely still, admiring every detail. Phia's Boutique was always dressed perfectly, with the best window displays ever. It made people smile when they walked by.

- Phia's Boutique -

open

The turquoise and gold trimmings on the window panes, the giant pink teacup, and the floral carpet - every detail a party for her eyes. But above all, she had never seen such a beautiful dress in all her life. It stood right in the middle of the store and looked as if it were dancing around the teacup. She loved the white tutu and floral top. "I would braid my hair into a crown and decorate it with beautiful flowers that smell like spring," Sarah thought to herself. She had always loved flowers and crowns.

"Oh Mom, please, pretty please can I have that dress?" Sarah pleaded. "That certainly is a beautiful dress, Sarah, and I can picture you wearing it," answered her mom. "But in the meantime, I think you can learn to wear patience." "Where do I buy patience?" Sarah answered with a cheeky grin. She remembered when she was younger and had asked her mom to take her to the shop that sold patience.

Mom smiled. "Remember, we cannot buy patience. It is something that we grow and practice. We can have patience because we know that every good thing comes from God, and His timing is perfect." Sarah wanted to ask just one more time for the dress, but she trusted her mom, and she felt strangely reassured.

The next morning Sarah couldn't wait to get to school, to tell Esther about the beautiful dress she had found to wear to her birthday party. The whole day at school she searched eagerly for Esther, but she couldn't find her. This year they were in separate classes, but they still exchanged a quick hug and chat as they passed each other at school. Esther also loved beautiful clothes, and she was sure to love the dress! Sarah was bursting with excitement at the idea of telling her friend about her dress.

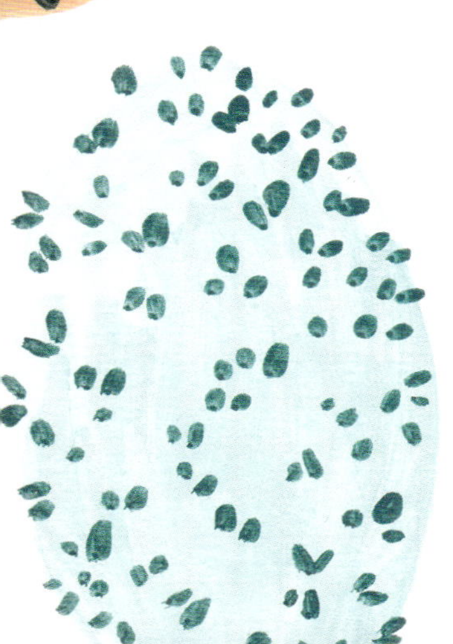

Finally, school ended and Sarah walked towards her mom's car. She was still dreaming of the fabulously spectacular entrance she would make at her party, wearing her exquisite princess dress. "I'm sure it's sewn with real gold," she was thinking to herself when she was interrupted by the familiar sound of Esther's voice. "Sarah! I have found the best dress to wear to your party!" Sarah ran up to her dear friend, "That's amazing, Esther. I've found one too, only I have to grow patience before I can get it." To remind them both, she quickly added, "Mom says patience grows when we have to wait for something that we really, really want."

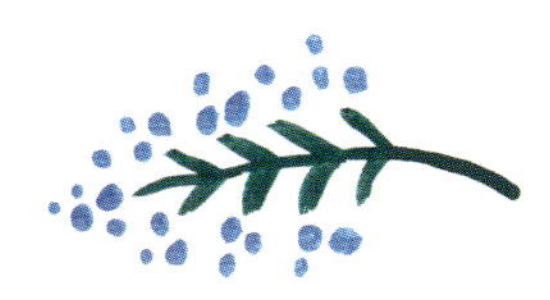

"So I don't have to grow patience to eat my vegetables?" Esther remarked, pulling her face as if she could taste them. "Nope, no patience needed there! I guess it's like waiting for your birthday, or for your tooth to fall out. So patience is like a little seed planted in your heart, and knowing that God is good and in control is what waters that seed," Sarah said, making sense of her mother's words as she repeated them to her friend.

"Thank you, Sarah. You always make my heart sparkle with your encouraging words," said Esther. "I don't actually have a dress to wear to your party. I only saw one in the window of Phia's Boutique and I really wanted it, but my mom said I should wait." Esther paused briefly and then added, "Oh, please would you help me to be patient?"

"Sarah, are you ok?" Mom instinctively knew whenever Sarah was feeling down. "Mom, Esther is going to buy my beautiful dream dress from Phia's Boutique. I don't think patience is a good thing at all. It's made me miss out."

"I understand that you feel that way because you really want that dress," said Sarah's mom. "But I also know that you love Esther, and your friendship is more important than any dress. A dress can tear or be thrown away, but a friend will be with you forever. Your words make your friends' hearts sparkle, and now your actions can make them shine." Sarah knew her mom was right.

The next morning Sarah thought to herself, "Today is my birthday. I might not get my dream dress, sewn with golden thread, but I do get to wear my gorgeous all-purpose dress that's perfect for any occasion!" Every morning, before Sarah jumped out of bed, she asked Jesus to dress her in love and joy. This was always her perfect outfit.

At last, it was party time! Each of her friends arrived carrying a hand-picked flower — they all knew how much Sarah loved flowers. They played and laughed and sipped tea elegantly from Mom's fine porcelain tea sets. They even lifted their pinkies to show what grand tea drinkers they were. It was perfect!

As everyone gathered around to sing happy birthday, Esther presented Sarah with a beautifully wrapped box. It was a large turquoise box with beautiful gold trimmings and a giant ribbon. Esther announced proudly, "This is from all your friends because you make us sparkle every day. Thank you for teaching me patience. It helped all of us to save our pocket money, to buy you something special." Sarah opened the box carefully and gently touched the soft tissue paper. She was overwhelmed by the familiar scent of roses, just as she remembered it at Phia's Boutique.

She carefully moved the tissue paper aside, and there it was: her beautiful dream dress! She felt overjoyed to touch the soft fabric, but she felt even more overjoyed that she had worn patience.

Now her dream dress would always be super special. Sarah leaned over to her mom and whispered, “Thank you, Mom, for teaching me to wear patience. It’s beautiful.”

CHECK YOUR HEART

- Do you like to go shopping with your mom or dad? If so, what are your favorite things to look at?

- How do you feel when your friend gets something or has something that you really want?

- Have you ever really wanted a new toy or dress, but your parents have told you that now is not the time? How did that make you feel?

HELP YOUR HEART

Sarah saw what she thought was her dream dress, and she really wanted it for her special party. Her mother also thought the dress was beautiful, but said she had to wait and be patient. God wants us to wear patience - trusting the right thing will happen because God is in control, and trusting our parents that they are making the right decision. Your thoughts could be telling you to start crying, yelling or even nagging for what you want. But God's patient girls know that He takes care of everything they need (Philippians 4:19). We should never feel we are going to miss out on something!

God's girls are patient - they celebrate with their friends. Friends love one another and are happy for them. (Romans 12:15)

God's girls are patient. Even when it doesn't seem like you will get the toy you so badly want. Your heart is made joyful because Jesus has given you a new day to sparkle in. (Psalms 118:24)

Patience is when I choose to let God help me accept with a happy heart that His time is always way better than my time. We choose to wear patience on the outside because our hearts are filled with trust for God on the inside. (Jeremiah 29:11)

BUILD YOUR HEART

- Read Philippians 4:6. When I pray about what I really want, I will protect my heart from impatience and keep on shining for Jesus while patiently waiting for His answer.

- Make a list of things you really want or have to wait for. Now pray and ask God to help you to keep to His time and not be impatient.

- Make a "patience" bracelet using alphabet beads and wear it with your favorite dress.

- Read about Sarah from the Bible in Genesis 17. She was a unique woman of faith; she too had to wear patience.

- Bake a cake with your mom or someone special. Remember to be patient because baking takes time. Patience will always have good results.